Farm Fun

Farm Machines

by Tessa Kenan

Bullfrog Books

Ideas for Parents and Teachers

Bullfrog Books let children practice reading informational text at the earliest reading levels. Repetition, familiar words, and photo labels support early readers.

Before Reading

- Discuss the cover photo. What does it tell them?
- Look at the picture glossary together. Read and discuss the words.

Read the Book

- "Walk" through the book and look at the pictures. Let the child ask questions. Point out the photo labels.
- Read the book to the child, or have him or her read independently.

After Reading

- Prompt the child to think more. Ask: Tractors do many jobs on the farm! They pull a lot of equipment. Have you seen a tractor?

Bullfrog Books are published by Jump!
5357 Penn Avenue South
Minneapolis, MN 55419
www.jumplibrary.com

Library of Congress Cataloging-in-Publication Data

Names: Kenan, Tessa, author.
Title: Farm machines / by Tessa Kenan.
Description: Minneapolis, MN: Jump!, Inc., [2021]
Series: Farm fun
Audience: Ages 5–8.
Audience: Grades K–1.
Identifiers: LCCN 2019055012 (print)
LCCN 2019055013 (ebook)
ISBN 9781645275251 (hardcover)
ISBN 9781645275268 (ebook)
Subjects: LCSH: Agricultural machinery—Juvenile literature. | Farms—Juvenile literature.
Classification: LCC S675.25 .K46 2021 (print)
LCC S675.25 (ebook) | DDC 631.3—dc23
LC record available at https://lccn.loc.gov/2019055012
LC ebook record available at https://lccn.loc.gov/2019055013

Editor: Jenna Gleisner
Designer: David Stavitzski

Photo Credits: stefan11/Shutterstock, cover, 1; Anatoliy Kosolapov/Shutterstock, 3; Sheryl Watson/Shutterstock, 4; oticki/Shutterstock, 5, 22; smereka/Shutterstock, 6–7, 13, 22; fotohalo/iStock, 8, 22; Romariolen/Shutterstock, 9; i-Stockr/iStock, 10–11, 22; wmaster890/iStock, 12, 22; Danita Delimont/Alamy, 14–15, 22; Lightpainter/Dreamstime, 16–17, 22; Steven Liveoak/Dreamstime, 18–19, 22; Aleksandar Varbenov/Dreamstime, 20–21; Stockr/Shutterstock, 23tl; DenBoma/iStock, 23bl; Dumitrescu Ciprian-Florin/Shutterstock, 24.

Printed in the United States of America at Corporate Graphics in North Mankato, Minnesota.

Table of Contents

Tractors Pull

What is this big machine?

A tractor!

Tractors are strong.

They do many farm jobs.

It is spring.

This one pulls a plow.

The plow digs up soil.

plow

soil

One pulls a planter.

planter

It drops seeds in rows.
Seeds grow into crops.
Nice!

sprayer

One pulls a sprayer.
It sprays bugs.
Why?
Bugs kill the crops.

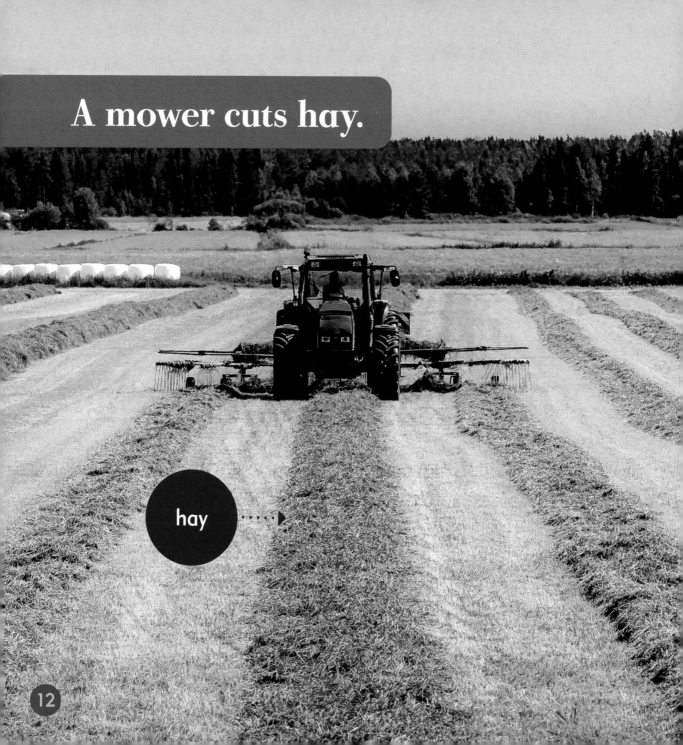

A mower cuts hay.

hay

baler

bale

A baler picks it up.
It makes bales.
Wow!

Fall is harvest time.
A combine cuts
down corn.

combine

grain
cart

Corn pours into
a grain cart.

Cool!

17

The cart pours it into a truck.

The truck will carry it to the farm.

Neat!

truck

The tractor pulls
a plow again.

Why?

This helps the soil
for next year!

21

Many Machines

Tractors and combines are big farm machines! Tractors pull many other machines. Take a look!

tractor

plow

planter

sprayer

mower

baler

combine

grain cart

grain truck

Picture Glossary

bales
Large bundles of things, such as hay or straw, that are tied tightly together.

harvest
To gather crops from a field.

hay
Long grass that is dried and used as food for farm animals.

soil
The top layer of Earth in which plants grow.

Index

To Learn More

Finding more information is as easy as 1, 2, 3.

❶ Go to www.factsurfer.com

❷ Enter "farmmachines" into the search box.

❸ Click the "Surf" button to see a list of websites.